<[A Math]~±÷
Journey Through
EXTREME SPORTS

Hilary Koll & Steve Mills

🌳 Crabtree Publishing Company
www.crabtreebooks.com

Crabtree Publishing Company
www.crabtreebooks.com
1-800-387-7650

Published in Canada
616 Welland Ave.
St. Catharines, ON
L2M 5V6

Published in the United States
PMB 59051, 350 Fifth Ave.
59th Floor,
New York, NY

First published in 2016 by Wayland
(A division of Hachette Children's Books)
Copyright © Wayland 2016

Authors: Hilary Koll and Steve Mills
Commissioning editor: Elizabeth Brent
Editors: Joe Fullman, Rob Colson, Kathy Middleton
  and Janine Deschenes
Proofreader: Petrice Custance
Math Consultant: Diane Dakers
Designer: Ed Simkins
Prepress technician: Katherine Berti
Print and production coordinator: Katherine Berti

Production coordinated by Tall Tree Ltd

Photographs:
iStockphoto: 4–5 MichaelSvoboda, 6 Sabonis, 8
DCorn, 9 Andrzej Burak, 10–11 LifeJourneys,
12–13 vm, 14–15 raclro, 16t MarcelC, 17t ZagE,
17b GibsonPictures, 18t and 19br Eduard
Andras, 20–21 gregepperson, 23 JaredAlden, 25
Jason Lugo, 26 4x6, 26–27 KeithBinns.
Dreamstime.com: 19t Salajean.
All other images by Shutterstock.

The website addresses (URLs) included in this
book were valid at the time of going to press.
However, it is possible that contents or
addresses may have changed since the
publication of this book. No responsibility for
any such changes can be accepted by either the
author or the Publisher.

Printed in Canada/022016/IH20151223

Library and Archives Canada Cataloguing in Publication

Koll, Hilary, author
        A math journey through extreme sports / Hilary Koll, Steve
Mills.

(Go figure!)
Includes index.
Issued in print and electronic formats.
ISBN 978-0-7787-2313-4 (bound).--
ISBN 978-0-7787-2325-7 (paperback).--
ISBN 978-1-4271-7717-9 (html)

        1. Mathematics--Juvenile literature. 2. Extreme sports--
Juvenile
literature. I. Mills, Steve, author II. Title.

QA40.5.K654 2016   j510   C2015-907937-3
                                        C2015-907938-1

Library of Congress Cataloging-in-Publication Data

Names: Koll, Hilary, author. | Mills, Steve, 1955- author.
Title: A math journey through extreme sports / Hilary Koll and Steve
    Mills.
Description: New York, New York : Crabtree Publishing, 2016. |
    "2016 | Series: Go figure! | Includes index. | Description based
    on print version record and CIP data provided by publisher;
    resource not viewed.
Identifiers: LCCN 2016001507 (print) | LCCN 2015049846 (ebook) |
    ISBN 9781427177179 (electronic HTML)
    ISBN 9780778723134 (reinforced library binding : alk. paper) |
    ISBN 9780778723257 (pbk. : alk. paper)
Subjects: LCSH: Mathematics--Juvenile literature. | Extreme sports--
    Juvenile literature.
Classification: LCC QA40.5 (print) | LCC QA40.5 .K655 2016 (ebook)
    | DDC 510--dc23
LC record available at http://lccn.loc.gov/2016001507

go figure!

Use your mathematical skills to explore the exciting world of extreme sports, solve puzzles and complete missions to turn you into an ace sports reporter.

CONTENTS

04 SKYRUNNING

06 SKELETON

08 HANG GLIDING

10 WINDSURFING

12 ICE CLIMBING

14 MOGUL SKIING

16 MOTOCROSS

18 CAVING

20 RAPPELLING

22 SLACKLINING

24 SNOWBOARDING

26 WAKEBOARDING

28 GO FIGURE! ANSWERS

30 MATH GLOSSARY

32 LEARNING MORE AND INDEX

Words in **bold** appear in the glossary on pages 30–31.

Answers to the Go Figure! challenges can be found on page 28.

Please note: The standard and metric systems are used interchangeably throughout this book.

WHAT EQUIPMENT DO YOU NEED?

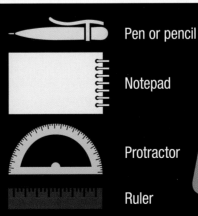

Pen or pencil

Notepad

Protractor

Ruler

You might find some of the questions in this book are too hard to do without the help of a calculator. Ask your teacher about when and how to use a calculator.

SKYRUNNING

Your first mission will take you up some of the world's highest mountains to try skyrunning. This extreme sport involves running races against other competitors at altitudes of more than 2000 meters. You're given a score for each race, which you add up over the season.

LEARN ABOUT IT
MENTAL ADDITION

04

There are lots of strategies to make adding lists of numbers in your head easier. Have you tried these?

Look for numbers in the list that can be added together to make 10 or a **multiple** of 10, such as $7 + 3$, $36 + 14$, $88 + 12$, and so on. This strategy can be used on both sides of this equation:

$$36 + 38 + 34 + 32 + 30 = 70 + 70 + 30$$
$$70 + 70 + 30 = 100 + 70$$
$$170 = 170$$

Another strategy is to add the Tens and Ones separately, especially if the Ones digits are small. To add 40, 42, 31, 62, and 51, first add their Tens: 40, 40, 30, 60, and 50, which equals 220. Then add on the Ones leftover from each number: 2, 1, 2, and 1. Adding these brings the total to 226.

In a third strategy, you can use multiplication if the numbers in the list being added are close to each other. For example, the numbers 44, 46, 44, 46, and 48 all have at least 44 in them. Multiply 44 by the number of numbers, which is 5.

Multiply by Tens first: $40 \times 5 = 200$
then by Ones: $\underline{4 \times 5 = 20}$
$= 220$

Then add the differences between the original numbers and 44, which is 2, 2, and 4. This brings the total to 228.

In a fourth strategy, round the numbers in the list to the nearest 10. For example, if the last digit is 5 or more, round the number up to the next multiple of 10. If it's 4 or less, round it down. To add 34, 88, 61, 27, and 59, first add their rounded numbers together: 30, 90, 60, 30, and 60 = 270. Then write down how much larger or smaller each number is than its rounded number:

34 is 4 more than 30, which we can write as +4
88 is 2 less than 90, which we can write as -2
61 is 1 more than 60, which we can write as +1
27 is 3 less than 30, which we can write as -3
59 is 1 less than 60, which we can write as -1

Next, adjust the total of rounded numbers by the differences:
$270 + 4 - 2 + 1 - 3 - 1 = 269$.

>GO FIGURE!

In each skyrunning season, competitors enter at least five races. Each competitor's best four results are added up, and the runner with the highest total is the champion. They win points according to where they finish:

1st – 100 points
2nd – 88 points
3rd – 78 points
4th – 72 points
5th – 68 points

After 5th, points go down by twos to the 40th position, which is 2 points.

RACE	COMPETITOR					
	Sam	Jo	Francis	Al	Alex	Jamie
Race 1 Spain, May 25	88	78	66	100	2	20
Race 2 Italy, June 21	78	100	66	42	88	64
Race 3 Switzerland, August 10	64	54	64	6	78	4
Race 4 Switzerland, August 28	88	38	62	74	100	78
Race 5 Italy, October 10	78	100	68	64	88	82

1. Figure out the total of Francis's five scores all together. Use one of the mental strategies suggested.

2. Now figure out the total of Jamie's five scores. Who scored the most points in the five races all together: Francis or Jamie?

3. For each competitor, write their lowest/worst score.

4. Taking only their best four scores and ignoring their worst score, find the total for each competitor.

5. Which of the competitors has the highest score and should be crowned champion?

05

SKELETON

Next, get your courage up to participate in the skeleton. In this dangerous sport, you travel on a special small sled at very high speeds—without brakes—along an icy track. Your nose is just centimeters from the ground!

LEARN ABOUT IT
DECIMALS

Decimals **are another way of writing fractions. For example, the grids below each have 100 squares. The number of colored squares can be represented as a number out of 100 or as a decimal.**

	fraction		decimal		
			ones	tenths	hundredths
two hundredths	$\frac{2}{100}$		0 .	0	2
one tenth	$\frac{10}{100}$		0 .	1	0
14 hundredths	$\frac{14}{100}$		0 .	1	4
113 hundredths	$\frac{113}{100}$		1 .	1	3

When comparing decimals, remember that the **place value** to the right of the decimal point becomes smaller as you move column to column from left to right. So, you must start by comparing the left-hand columns after the decimal. The column to the right of the hundredths column would be thousandths, and so on.

When comparing numbers, it helps if the numbers have the same number of digits after the decimal point. To do this, we can write zeros in the end positions that have no digits. For example, one tenth can be written as either 0.1 or 0.10. Written both ways, each has 1 tenth and 0 hundredths. But adding a zero makes it easier to see that 0.10 lies between 0.02 and 0.14, as in the example above.

Let's use the extra zeros to put these numbers in order: 1.3, 1.25, and 1.287. This makes it easy to see that 1.300 is the largest, followed by 1.287, and then 1.250.

>GO FIGURE!

There are only a few official skeleton ice tracks around the world. They have varying lengths and vertical drops, and have different numbers of curves.

	Country	Track	Length (km)	Vertical drop (m)	Curves
	Austria	Igls	1.22	98.1	14
	Russia	Paramonovo	1.6	105	19
	Russia	Sochi	1.814	131.9	19
	Canada	Calgary	1.475	121.48	14
	Canada	Whistler	1.45	152	16
	Germany	Königssee	1.306	117	13
	Germany	Winterberg	1.33	110	14
	Germany	Oberhof	1.069	96.37	15
	Germany	Altenberg	1.413	122.22	17
	United States	Lake Placid	1.455	107	20
	United States	Park City	1.34	103.9	15
	Switzerland	St. Moritz	1.722	130	16
	Latvia	Sigulda	1.2	111.5	16
	France	La Plagne	1.507	119	19
	Japan	Nagano	1.36	113	14
	Italy	Cortina d'Ampezzo	1.35	120.45	13
	Norway	Lillehammer	1.365	114.3	16

1 Look at the lengths of the first two tracks above. Which is longer?

2 Which of the two Canadian tracks
a) has the longer length;
b) has the longer vertical drop;
c) has more curves?

3 Put Germany's four tracks in order of length, starting with the longest.

4 Which of all the tracks
a) is the longest;
b) has the greatest vertical drop;
c) has the most curves?

HANG GLIDING

So far, you've been running up mountains and traveling on ice. Your next mission is to leave Earth and head up into the air to compare hang gliding (using a device like a kite) and paragliding (using a device like a parachute). For this you need to know about **ratios**.

LEARN ABOUT IT

RATIOS AND SIMILAR TRIANGLES

Ratios compare two or more things. In this tile pattern, for example, there is one black tile for every eight white tiles. We write the ratio of black tiles to white tiles as 1:8.

08

Ratios can be multiplied or divided to show the same basic relationship. For example, the ratio **1:8** is the same ratio as **2:16** (1 × 2 : 8 × 2), or **3:24** (1 × 3 : 8 × 3), or even **100:800** (1 × 100 : 8 × 100). Of all of these ratios, 1:8 is in the **simplest form** because the numbers have been reduced to the smallest numbers possible.

Triangles whose sides are in the same ratio are called similar triangles. The first triangle below measures 6 squares across and 2 down. It has the ratio **6:2**.

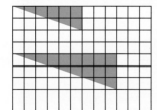

The second triangle measures 9 squares across and 3 down, giving it the ratio **9:3**. These are similar triangles because both ratios can be written as **3:1** in their simplest forms, as shown below:

It is also easier to compare ratios when the second number is simplified to 1, so that the ratio can be written in the form **n:1**. To do this, divide both numbers in the ratio by the second number. After it is divided, the "n," or first number, might end up as a decimal.

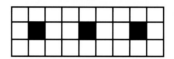

6:2
÷2   ÷2
3:1

9:3
÷3   ÷3
3:1

7:2
÷2   ÷2
3.5:1

17:4
÷4   ÷4
4.25:1

❯GO FIGURE!

Hang gliding and paragliding are described using glide ratios. For instance, gliding 12 m forward for every 1 m of height you come down is the glide ratio 12:1. Paragliders can have glide ratios of up to 10:1, while hang gliders can have ratios of up to 20:1. Compare the ratios below and answer the questions.

three paragliding flights

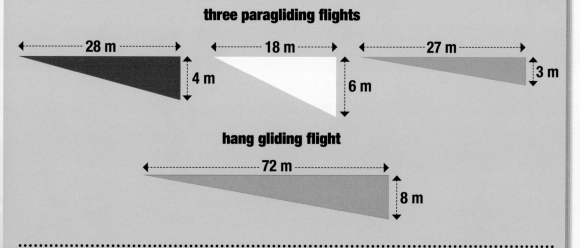

hang gliding flight

① Write the glide ratio of each paragliding flight in its simplest form.

② Which of the three paragliding flights (pink, yellow or blue) has the same glide ratio as the hang gliding flight?

③ Write each of the following ratios in the form n:1.
a) 35 m across for every 5 m down;
b) 15 m across for every 2 m down;
c) 113 m across for every 10 m down;
d) 41 m across for every 4 m down.

④ Which of the ratios in question 3 travels the farthest across for each meter of drop?

WINDSURFING

The extreme sport of windsurfing isn't just about racing across the waves as fast as you can. The speed of the wind, your own body weight, and the size of your sail all affect your performance.

LEARN ABOUT IT
AREA

Area is the amount of surface that something has. Area is measured in squares, such as square centimeters (cm²) or square meters (m²).

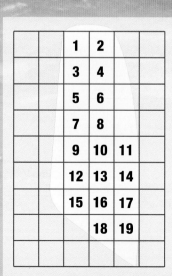

We can count area on a grid of squares. For an irregular shape, such as a sail, we can estimate its area by counting the whole squares first, and then imagine joining the part squares together to make whole squares. For the sail on the grid at left, we could estimate about 24 squares (19 whole squares and roughly 5 more squares from parts).

When windsurfing sails are made, their area is calculated very accurately in square meters.

›GO FIGURE!

This table shows the best sail areas for different windsurfer body weights and wind speeds. The sections in yellow indicate sail sizes that are impractical or not available.

Wind speed in knots

Windsurfer weight in kg	10	14	18	22	26	30	34	38
50	6.7	4.8	3.7	3	2.6	2.2	2	1.8
60	8	5.7	4.5	3.7	3.1	2.7	2.4	2.1
70	9.4	6.7	5.2	4.3	3.5	3.1	2.8	2.4
80	10.7	7.7	6	4.9	4.1	3.6	3.2	2.8
90	12.1	8.6	6.7	5.5	4.6	4	3.5	3.2
100	13.4	9.6	7.4	6.1	5.2	4.5	3.9	3.5
110	14.7	10.5	8.2	6.7	5.7	4.9	4.3	3.9

Ideal sail size (area) in m²

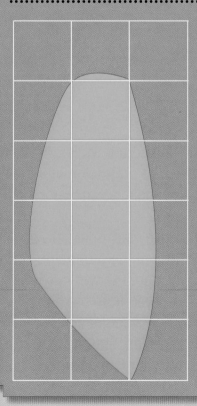

1. Estimate the area of the blue sail on the left, if each square represents 1 m².

2. Given a wind speed of 22 knots, what is the ideal sail size for someone weighing:
   a) 50 kg,   b) 80 kg, c) 110 kg?

3. James weighs 90 kg. What sail size is ideal for him when the wind speed is:
   a) 14 knots, b) 26 knots, c) 38 knots?

4. A windsurfing club has a sail with an area of 6.7 m². Is the sail ideal for any of the following riders in the conditions shown?

   • Sam, who weighs 50 kg, in a wind speed of 18 knots?

   • Lucy, who weighs 70 kg, in a wind speed of 14 knots?

   • Clive, who weighs 110 kg, in a wind speed of 22 knots?

ICE CLIMBING

Ice climbers use special tools called ice axes to dig into giant frozen walls and haul themselves up to the top. Walls that are vertical or overhanging (jutting out more than 90°) are the most challenging to climb, while less steep slopes (as small as 60°) are easier.

LEARN ABOUT IT
ANGLE AND SCALE DRAWINGS

Angles **are measured in degrees (°). We measure angles with a tool called a** protractor**, like the one shown below.**

An angle that is 90 degrees (90°) is called a right angle.

An angle less than 90° is called an **acute angle**.

Angles between 90° and 180° are called **obtuse angles**.

60°   90°   110°

To measure and draw angles, line up the center of the protractor with the corner of the angle, as shown left.

Be careful to start from zero on each side of the protractor. The example shown here is measured from the right side in a counterclockwise direction. Starting at zero, this angle measures 50° (not 130°).

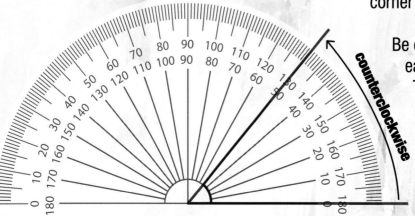

When drawing pictures of real-life objects, we use a **scale**, which is a ratio that shows how the lengths or distances on the drawing relate to the real size. For example, 1 cm in a picture can represent 500 cm in real life. We would write the scale as the ratio 1:500. A scale drawing also has the same angles as the real-life object. Tip: To answer the questions below, it's helpful to remember that 100 cm = 1m and 500 cm = 5 m.

›GO FIGURE!

Different ice climbs are given different grades by climbers that describe the slope and length of the climb. Compare these drawings, noting the different scales, then answer the questions below.

Climb A
Scale 1:100

Climb B
Scale 1:800

1. Use a protractor to measure the angle for each ice climb.

2. Use a ruler to measure the length of each of the walls from the corner of the angle to the highest point. Round up your answers to the nearest cm.

3. Use the scales to figure out the actual length of each climb in real life.

4. List the four climbs in order starting with the one you think is easiest, and ending with the hardest climb.

Climb C
Scale 1:600

Climb D
Scale 1:1000

MOGUL SKIING

Your next extreme sport to research is mogul skiing, which involves skiing down a course around mounds, called moguls, and flying off bumps. Judges decide on the score for each skier based on their speed and how they perform the turns and air jumps.

LEARN ABOUT IT
PERCENTAGES

Some skills in mogul skiing are more difficult than others. When a competitor's scores are added together, each score is weighted**, or given a** percentage **that reflects the skill's difficulty.**

Think of a percentage as the numerator, or top number, in a fraction in which the denominator, or bottom number, is 100. Fifty is half of 100. So, to find 50% of a number, divide the number by 2. Twenty-five is one quarter of 100, so divide your number by 4 to find 25%.

100%		
50%	25%	25%

To find 10 percent of a number, divide it by 10.
To find 20 percent of a number, divide it by 5,
(or divide it by 10 and then double the answer).
To find 60 percent of a number, divide it by 10 and then multiply the answer by 6.

100%		
60%	20%	20%

When finding a final weighted score, you need to apply the percentage for each score first, and then add the answers together to give a final score. For example, i† a skier scores 20 for a skill that has a percentage weight of 10%, the amount from that score that would be added to the skier's final score would be: **20 ÷ 10 = 2**.

>GO FIGURE!

Calculate the final scores to answer the questions below based on the percentage weightings listed in this chart. You may find it useful to use a calculator.

In the first competition, the scores are rated as follows:
Turns 50% • Air jumps 25% • Speed 25%

100%		
Turns	Air Jumps	Speed

In the second competition, they are rated as follows:
Turns 60% • Air jumps 20% • Speed 20%

100%		
Turns	Air Jumps	Speed

1 Kasper scored 30 points in turns, 20 points in air jumps, and 12 points in speed. What would his final score be if he was in:
a) the first competition,
b) the second competition?

2 Which weighting works better for Kasper?

3 Kayley scored 20 points in turns, 28 points in air jumps, and 13 points in speed. What would her final score be if she was in:
a) the first competition,
b) the second competition?

4 Which weighting works better for Kayley?

15

MOTOCROSS

Motocross bikes are specially designed to travel over rough, bumpy tracks. For your next mission, you need to learn how the size of the wheels affect performance in this extreme sport.

LEARN ABOUT IT CIRCLES

Wheels are basically circles. You can figure out the radius, diameter, **and** circumference **of a wheel in the same way you can for a circle.**

The radius of a circle is the distance from the edge to the center of the circle. It is half the length of the diameter, which is the widest distance across the circle, through the center. The circumference is the **perimeter** of the circle, or the distance all the way around its edge.

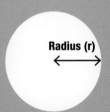
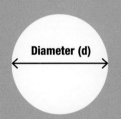
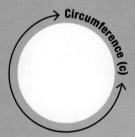

There is a special relationship between the diameter (d) of a circle and its circumference (c). For every circle, the circumference will always be 3.14 times the diameter. The number 3.14 is called **pi**, and its mathematical symbol is π. Pi is a never-ending number, so it is usually rounded to 3.14. The **formula** for circumference can be written as $c = \pi \times d$.

You can use the circumference of a wheel to figure out how far a bike has traveled. Imagine a spot of paint on the tire leaving a series of marks on the track as it rolls. In this example, the wheel has turned 3 full rotations, so the distance it has traveled would be 3 × its circumference, or 3c.

circumference

>GO FIGURE!

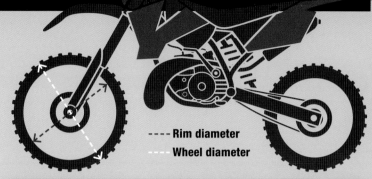

The front and rear wheels on motocross bikes are different sizes. The engine drives the back wheel, and each wheel rotates at a different rate. So, one wheel might make five turns in the same time that the other wheel makes four.

Tip for answering questions below:
100 cm = 1 m.

- - - - Rim diameter
- - - - Wheel diameter

WHEEL	RIM DIAMETER (WITHOUT THE TIRE)	WHEEL DIAMETER (WITH THE TIRE)
FRONT	40.6 cm	53.2 cm
REAR	35.5 cm	49.0 cm

1. How much larger is: a) the rim diameter of the front wheel than the rear wheel, b) the wheel diameter of the front wheel than the rear wheel?

2. Taking π to be 3.14, calculate the circumference of:
a) the front wheel with tire,
b) the rear wheel with tire.

3. Giving your answer in meters, how far would the motorbike go if:

a) the front wheel makes 10 turns while in contact with the ground without slipping,
b) the rear wheel makes 10 turns while in contact with the ground without slipping?

4. Without leaving the ground or slipping, how many times would:
a) the front wheel turn in 585.2 m,
b) the rear wheel turn in 585.2 m?

CAVING

Cavers, or spelunkers, explore networks of caves and cracks below ground level. This can involve rappelling down walls using rope, crawling through tight cracks, swimming underwater, and rock climbing.

LEARN ABOUT IT
COORDINATES AND NEGATIVE NUMBERS

A cave can be mapped using a grid. The grid can be divided by two lines called the x-axis (horizontal) and the y-axis (vertical). They divide the grid into four areas called quadrants. **The origin is where the x-axis meets the y-axis.**

18

Any point on the grid can be referred to by its coordinates. All coordinates are measured starting from the origin. Coordinates are written as two numbers inside brackets, separated by a comma. The first number shows you the distance you have to go from the origin to the left or right across the x-axis to get to a location. The second number shows the distance you have to go up or down on the y-axis.

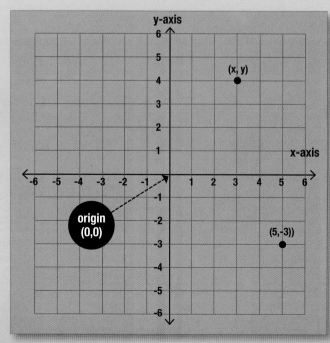

The point (x,y) on the grid to the left is at (3,4). This means you go 3 squares to the right from the origin, and 4 squares up to reach the point.

All points on the right of the y-axis have positive x values. All points on the left of the y-axis have negative x values. All points above the x-axis have positive y values. All points below the x-axis have negative y values. So, the point (5,-3) is 5 squares to the right of the y-axis and 3 below the x-axis.

❭GO FIGURE!

You have mapped out the cave you just explored. Use your knowledge of coordinates and **negative numbers** to figure out routes through the cave system.

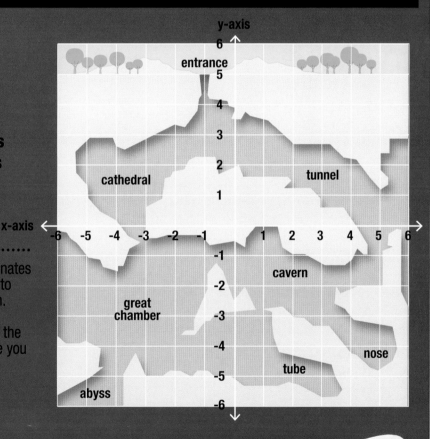

1 Write the coordinates of the entrance to the cave system.

2 In which part of the cave system are you if you are at:
a) (-4,2)
b) (-4,-3)
c) (3,-5)
d) (5,-4)
e) (-6,-6)?

3 Follow this route from the entrance, and see where you end up.
down 2, right 2, down 1, right 3, down 1, right 1, down 3, left 3.

4 Describe a route to get from (2,-2) to the abyss.

RAPPELLING

Rappelling is a method of climbing down a cliff face or the side of a building using a rope and harness to control how quickly you descend. The rope is secured at the top of whatever you are climbing. Your mission is to climb several tall places and take measurements.

LEARN ABOUT IT
RIGHT-ANGLED TRIANGLES AND TANGENTS

It is possible to figure out the height of a tall building or cliff and never have to leave the ground to do it.

The base of the building or cliff, its top, and you represent the three vertices, or points, of a **right-angled triangle**. If you know how far away you are standing from the object's base (distance, or **d**), and you can measure the angle from where you are standing to the top of it (angle, or **a**), you can find the object's height.

The formula showing how to find the height (**h**) is:

$$h = \tan(a) \times d$$

Tan is the short form found on scientific calculators for the term **tangent**. The tangent shows the relationship between the angle and two of the sides of a right-angled triangle.

You can find a scientific calculator by doing a search on the Internet. (First make sure the "degrees" button is set on the calculator, not the "radians" button.) Try this example: if the angle, **a**, is 30°, and the distance, **d**, is 400 m, then we find the height on the calculator by keying in: "tan (30) =", then "× 400 =".
The answer is 230.9401077 m. A long decimal answer can be rounded to one decimal place: 230.9 m.

›GO FIGURE!

You visit some different places to rappel down and take lots of measurements. These sketches show your measurements. Let's see which of the descents was the most challenging!

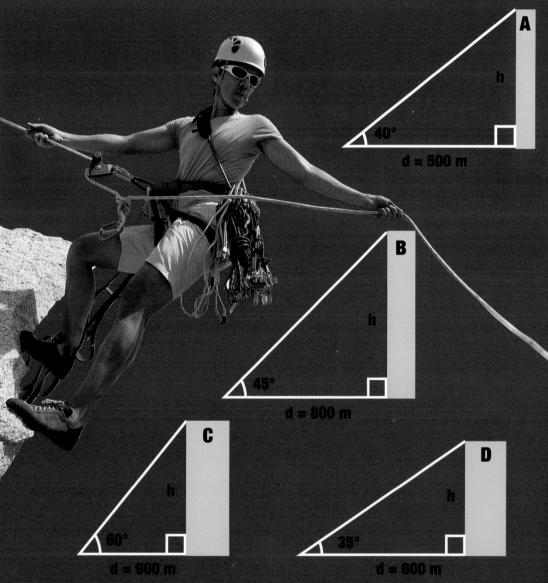

A
h
40°
d = 500 m

B
h
45°
d = 800 m

C
h
60°
d = 900 m

D
h
35°
d = 600 m

---

1 Giving each answer to one decimal place, find the height, **h**, for: a) skyscraper A, b) skyscraper B, c) cliff C, d) building D.

2 Which two descents are a similar height?

3 What do you notice about **d** and **h** for skyscraper B?

4 Which of the descents is the: a) largest, b) smallest?

SLACKLINING

Slacklining is similar to tightrope walking, but it's done on a stretchy line, like a very thin trampoline. World records for the highest and longest crossings around the world were recorded using different units of measurement. Your mission is to convert them all to metric for easy comparison.

LEARN ABOUT IT
MEASUREMENT CONVERSIONS

When comparing measurements, it is important to know the relationships between units, like this:

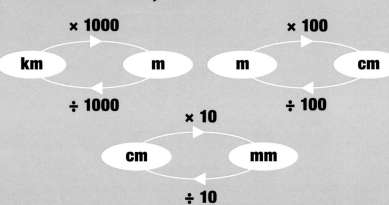

Remember to check whether the units of the measurements you are comparing are the same. Here, they are all different. We need to change them all to meters by multiplying or dividing by 1,000, 100 or 10, using the diagrams above for reference.

6 km	57,300 cm	100,000 mm
× 1000	÷ 100	÷ 10 = 10,000 cm, then ÷ 100
6000 m	573 m	100 m

Lengths are also given in imperial. Their relationships to metric units are shown at right. Use multiplication and division to convert from one to the other, as shown in the examples below:

500 inches = 500 in × 2.5 cm = 1,250 cm

3.2 km = 3.2 km ÷ 1.6 km × 1 mile = 2 miles

Length

1 inch ≈ 2.5 cm
12 inches = 1 foot ≈ 30 cm
3 feet = 1 yard ≈ 90 cm
1760 yards = 1 mile ≈ 1.6 km

≈ means "approximately equal to"

22

>GO FIGURE!

These are the world slacklining records. They include highlining, which is slacklining over a big drop, and waterlining, which is slacklining over water. Measurements are given in different units.

RECORD	DISTANCE	PERSON	PLACE	DATE
Longest slackline (men)	2000 feet long	Alexander Schulz	Inner Mongolia, China	May 2015
Longest slackline (women)	23,000 cm long	Laetitia Gonnon	Lausanne, Switzerland	September 2014
Highest ever slackline	1.2 km high	Andy Lewis	Mojave desert, Nevada, USA	March 2014
Highest urban highline	185 m high	Reinhard Kleindl	Frankfurt, Germany	May 2013
Longest waterline	363 yards long	Alexander Schulz	Eibsee, Denmark	August 2014
Longest highline (men)	1230 feet long	Alexander Schulz	Yangshuo, China	November 2014
Longest highline (women)	105 m long	Faith Dickey	Moab, Utah USA	November 2014

1. What is the men's longest slackline record: a) in centimeters, b) in meters?

2. What is the women's longest slackline record: a) in meters, b) in kilometers?

3. What is the difference between the highest-ever slackline record and the highest urban slackline record, in meters?

4. Convert the longest waterline record into meters.

5. a) Convert the men's longest highline record into meters.
b) How much longer is the men's highline record than the women's record, in meters?

SNOWBOARDING

For your next mission, you must judge halfpipe snowboarding. In a halfpipe competition, snowboarders do tricks down a pipe-shaped course. The scoring system is quite complicated, so make sure you correctly figure out who the winner is!

LEARN ABOUT IT
MEAN, MEDIAN, AND MODE AVERAGES

Averages summarize a set of numbers using just one number. There are different types of averages, including the mean, the median, and the mode.

To calculate the mean average of a set of numbers, find the total of all the values, and then divide it by how many numbers there are.

For example, to find the mean average of 44, 57, 42, 49, and 58, add them together, then divide the answer by how many numbers there are in the set (5).

$$44 + 57 + 42 + 49 + 58 = 250$$

$$250 \div 5 = 50$$

The mean average of this set of numbers is 50.

The median average is found by writing the numbers in order and selecting the middle value. For example, 44, 57, 42, 49 and 58 can be written in order as:

$$42, 44, 49, 57, 58$$

The median is the middle value: 49.

The mode can be used when there is a lot of data and numbers are repeated. The mode is the number that occurs most often in a list of numbers:

$$3, 6, 3, 5, 6, 4, 6, 3, 4, 3, 4, 6, 7, 3, 3,$$
$$3, 5, 3, 7, 8, 2, 3, 7, 1, 3, 5, 3, 6, 6, 7$$

The mode is 3 because it occurs more times than any other number.

>GO FIGURE!

In halfpipe snowboarding, usually three to six judges each give a competitor a maximum of 100 points. If there are six judges, the middle four scores are averaged using the mean.

Judges score each rider based on:

- **Flow**—how fluid, or flawless, is the rider during tricks, landing, and movement through the course?

- **Creativity of line**—how much creativity does the rider put into their halfpipe?

- **Technical difficulty**—how hard are the moves and how well are they being performed?

- **Amplitude**—how high are the tricks?

- **Style**—the hardest to judge, but the most important.

Below are the basic scores for this competition from six judges. You must figure out the final scores of each rider.

NAME	J1	J2	J3	J4	J5	J6	Total of middle four scores	Mean score
Zhang Shi	67	73	75	78	86	70		
Ivan Plotchedov	83	88	86	85	88	94		
David Jenner	91	86	85	93	94	92		
Amru Szalji	86	89	87	88	90	88		
Andreas Schultz	94	95	92	95	98	95		
Kyle Robertson	96	98	96	97	97	95		

1. In snowboarding, the highest and lowest scores are removed. Find the total of the middle four scores for each competitor.

2. Divide each total by 4 to find the mean score, giving each as a decimal with 2 decimal places.

3. Write the competitors in order to complete a final winning table, with the highest mean score in first position.

4. Who wins the: a) gold medal, b) silver medal, c) bronze medal?

WAKEBOARDING

In wakeboarding, the competitor stands on a board and rides along the surface of the water, towed behind a motorboat. Depending on the size of the board, the rider's weight, the type of tricks, and the rider's comfort, they reach speeds of 30–40 kph (18–25 mph). Your final mission is to have some high-speed fun!

LEARN ABOUT IT
ANGLES AND SPEED

When wakeboarding, your board can turn—hopefully with you on it!

Angles are measured in degrees (°), with **90°** being a quarter turn, **180°** being a half turn, and **360°** being a full turn.

26

90°

180°

360°

Speeds of fast motorboats are usually measured in kilometers per hour (kph) or miles per hour (mph). One mile equals about 1.6 km. To convert (approximately) between units, use these formulas:

mph speed × 1.6 = kph speed	**kph speed ÷ 1.6 = mph speed**

35 mph × 1.6 = 56 kph   88 kph ÷ 1.6 = 55 mph

When solving problems in your head, it's easier to use these handy tricks:

mph speed ÷ 5 × 8 = kph speed	**kph speed ÷ 8 × 5 = mph speed**

You can see the answers in the examples below are the same as the answers in the first formulas:

35 mph ÷ 5 = 7, 7 × 8 = 56 kph   88 kph ÷ 8 = 11, 11 × 5 = 55 mph

Use this description of a wakeboarder's ride to answer questions about tricks and speed.

"At the start, the boat was going at an initial speed of 20 mph but sped up to about 40 km/h so I could do some spins. I started with a "Frontside 360" spin, which is doing a 360° rotation while in the air with my front toward the boat. I then did a "Backside 540" off the wake (wave of the boat) where I spin with the back of my body toward the boat first through 540°. I then did a "Backside 720." I tried an "Off-axis 900" spin where my board goes above shoulder level while I do a 900° rotation, but I haven't perfected it yet. I did a "Shifty" next, going 90° in one direction and then 90° back in the other. My aim is to do a "1080" spin by doing a 1080° rotation in the air, but I'm still working toward it."

27

....

1. What was the initial speed in kph?

2. How many miles per hour did the boat speed up to?

3. How many quarter turns in: a) the first part of a "Shifty," b) a "Frontside 360"?

4. How many half turns in a: a) "Frontside 360," b) "Backside 540," c) "Backside 720"?

5. Giving fractions in your answers if necessary, write how many full turns there are in a) "Backside 540," b) "Backside 720," c) "Off-axis 900," d) "1080 spin"?

GO FIGURE! ANSWERS

04–05 Skyrunning
1. 66 + 66 + 64 + 62 + 68 = 326
2. 20 + 64 + 4 + 78 + 82 = 248
   Francis scored more points.
3. Sam 64, Jo 38, Francis 62, Al 6,
   Alex 2, Jamie 4
4. Sam 332, Jo 332, Francis 264,
   Al 280, Alex 354, Jamie 244
5. Alex is the champion.

06–07 Skeleton
1. Paramonovo is longer (1.60 km)
   than Igls (1.22 km)
2. a) Calgary is the longest
   b) Whistler has the longer
   vertical drop
   c) Whistler has more curves
3. Alterberg (1.413 km), Winterberg
   (1.330 km), Königssee (1.306 km),
   Oberhof (1.069 km)
4. a) Sochi (1.814 km)
   b) Whistler (152 m)
   c) Lake Placid (20 curves)

08–09 Hang gliding
1. 28:4 = 7:1 18:6 = 3:1 27:3 = 9:1
2. 72:8 = 9:1 the blue triangle has
   the same glide ratio.
3. a) 35:5 = 7:1 b) 15:2 = 7.5:1
   c) 113:10 = 11.3:1
   d) 41:4 = 10.25:1
4. Glide path c) is the most
   impressive, with a ratio
   of 11.3:1

10–11 Windsurfing
1. Between 7 m^2 and 8 m^2 would be
   a good estimate.
2. a) 3 m^2 b) 4.9 m^2 c) 6.7 m^2
3. a) 8.6 m^2 b) 4.6 m^2 c) 3.2 m^2
4. Lucy and Clive

12–13 Ice climbing
1. a) 65°, b) 90°, c) 85°, d) 105°
2. a) 7 cm b) 5 cm c) 6 cm d) 5 cm
3. a) 7 × 100 = 700 cm = 7 m
   b) 5 × 800 = 4000 cm = 40 m
   c) 6 × 600 = 3600 cm = 36 m
   d) 5 × 1000 = 5000 cm = 50 m
4. A, C, B, D

14–15 Mogul skiing
1. a) (50% of 30) + (25% of 20) +
   (25% of 12) = 23
   b) (60% of 30) + (20% of 20) +
   (20% of 12) = 24.4
2. The second competition
3. a) (50% of 20) + (25% of 28) +
   (25% of 13) = 20.25
   b) (60% of 20) + (20% of 28) +
   (20% of 13) = 20.2
4. The first competition

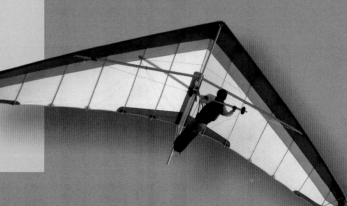

16–17 Motocross

1. a) 40.6 − 35.5 = 5.1 cm
   b) 53.2 − 49.0 = 4.2 cm
2. a) 3.14 × 53.2 = 167 cm
   b) 3.14 × 49.0 = 153.9 cm
3. a) 10 × 1.67 = 16.7 m
   b) 10 × 1.54 = 15.4 m
4. a) 585.2 ÷ 1.67 = 350
   b) 585.2 ÷ 1.54 = 380

18–19 Caving

1. (-1,5)
2. a) cathedral, b) great chamber,
   c) tube, d) nose, e) abyss
3. You would be at point (2,-2)
   in the part called "cavern."
4. Answers will vary, but can go left 2, up 1,
   left 3, down 3, left 1, down 2, left 1.

20–21 Rappelling

1. a) tan (40) × 500 = 419.5 m
   b) tan (45) × 800 = 800.0 m
   c) tan (60) × 900 = 1558.8 m
   d) tan (35) × 600 = 420.1 m
2. A and D
3. Both the distance from the base and the
   height are the same. This is because the
   triangle is an isosceles triangle with
   angles 45°, 45°, and 90°.
4. a) C is the largest at 1558.8 m.
   b) A is the smallest at 419.5 m.

22–23 Slacklining

1. a) 2000 × 30 = 60,000 cm
   b) 60,000 ÷ 100 = 600 m
2. a) 23,000 ÷ 100 = 230 m
   b) 230 ÷ 1000 = 0.23 km
3. 1.2 km = 1200 m , 1200 − 185 = 1015 m
4. 363 × 0.9 = 326.7 m

5. a) 1230 ÷ 8 = 410 yards
      410 × 0.9 = 369 m
   b) 369 − 105 = 264 m longer

24–25 Snowboarding

1. Zhang Shi = 296
   Ivan Plotchedov = 347
   David Jenner = 362
   Amru Szalji = 352
   Andreas Shultz = 379
   Kyle Robertson = 386
2. Zhang Shi = 296 ÷ 4 = 74
   Ivan Plotchedov = 347 ÷ 4 = 86.75
   David Jenner = 362 ÷ 4 = 90.50
   Amru Szalji = 352 ÷ 4 = 88.00
   Andreas Shultz = 379 ÷ 4 = 94.75
   Kyle Robertson = 386 ÷ 4 = 96.50
3. Kyle Robertson 96.50
   Andreas Schultz 94.75
   David Jenner 90.50
   Amru Szalji 88.00
   Ivan Plotchedov 86.75
   Zhang Shi 74
4. a) Kyle Robertson
   b) Andreas Schultz
   c) David Jenner

26–27 Wakeboarding

1. 20 ÷ 5 = 4, 4 × 8 = 32 kph
2. 40 ÷ 8 = 5, 5 × 5 = 25 mph
3. a) one quarter turn
   b) four quarter turns
4. a) two half turns
   b) three half turns
   c) four half turns
5. a) 540 ÷ 360 = 1½
   b) 720 ÷ 360 = 2
   c) 900 divided by 360 = 2½
   d) 1080 divided by 360 = 3

MATH GLOSSARY

ACUTE ANGLE
An angle that is less than 90°

ANGLE
The amount of turn, measured in degrees (°). There are 360 degrees in one full turn.

AREA
The amount of two-dimensional space covered by a shape or object. For example, the area of a rectangle is calculated by multiplying the length of one of the short sides by the length of one of the long sides.

CIRCUMFERENCE
The perimeter of a circle, which is the distance all the way around its edge

DECIMAL
A number with a decimal point in it. The digit to the left of the decimal point is the number of units, while the digit to the right is the number of tenths.

DIAMETER
The widest length across a circle, passing through the center

FORMULA
A system of numbers, symbols, and letters used to describe a mathematical relationship

KNOT
The speed when traveling at 1 nautical mile per hour on water

MEAN AVERAGE
The average found by adding all the values and dividing by the number of values there are

MEDIAN
The middle value of a set of values arranged in order of size

MODE
The most common value in a set of values

MULTIPLE
The result of multiplying one number by another number

NEGATIVE NUMBER
Numbers that are below zero. We write them using the minus sign (-), e.g. -5, -3, -7.

OBTUSE ANGLE
An angle that is between 90° and 180°

PERCENTAGE
A percentage is a fraction with a denominator of 100, e.g. 42% = $^{42}/_{100}$. Per cent means "for every hundred."

PERIMETER
The total distance around a shape. It is calculated by adding together the lengths of all the shape's sides.

PI
Written as π, pi is a special number that is approximately 3.1412 or $^{22}/_7$. It is the relationship between the diameter and circumference of a circle.

PLACE VALUE
The value that a digit has based on where it appears in a number.

PROTRACTOR
A mathematical instrument, shaped in a circle or a semi-circle. It is marked with degrees and used to measure angles.

QUADRANT
One of the four sections created when a grid is divided by two lines that cross, such as the x-axis and y-axis

RADIUS
The distance between the center of a circle and its circumference.

RATIO
Ratios show how one or more numbers or values are related to another. So a ratio of 2:1 shows that there are twice as many of the first value as there are of the second.

RIGHT-ANGLED TRIANGLE
A triangle that has a right angle of 90° as one of its angles.

SCALE
A number that shows how much a map or drawing has been made smaller. For example, a scale of 1:100 means that the drawing is 100 times smaller than the original, so 1 cm on the drawing represents 100 cm, or 1 m, in real life.

SIMPLIFY/SIMPLEST FORM
To simplify a ratio, we change it to an equivalent ratio that uses smaller numbers, e.g. 4:12 = 1:3. When a number cannot be simplified, it is in its simplest form. Fractions can also be simplified in the same way, e.g. $^6/_8 = ^3/_4$.

TAN OR TANGENT
The tangent of an angle in a right-angled triangle is the relationship between the opposite side to the angle divided by the adjacent side (not the longest side, the hypotenuse).

WEIGHTED SCORE
A total score made by combining different scores, where some of the scores are more important than others.

LEARNING MORE

WEBSITES

www.mathisfun.com
A huge website packed full of explanations, examples, games, puzzles, activities, worksheets, and teacher resources for all age levels.

www.khanacademy.org
A learning resource website for all ages, it contains practice exercises and easy-to-follow instructional videos on all subjects, including math.

www.mathplayground.com
An action-packed website with math games, mathematical word problems, worksheets, puzzles, and videos.

INDEX

32

acute angle 12
addition 4
angles 12–13, 26–27
area 10–11
averages 24–25
axes 18

circles 16–17
circumference 16, 17
conversions 22–23, 26–27
coordinates 18–19

decimals 6, 20
diameter 16, 17

estimating areas 10–11

fractions 6

hundredths 6

imperial units 22

mean 24–25
measurements 22–23
median 24
mode 24
multiplication 4

negative numbers 18–19

obtuse angle 12
origin 18

percentages 14–15
pi (π) 16–17
protractor 12, 13

quadrants 18

radius 16
ratios 8–9
right angle 12, 20–21
right-angled triangles 20–21
rounding 5, 20

scale drawings 12–13
similar triangles 8–9
slopes 12, 13
speed 26–27
squares 10–11, 18

tangent (tan) 20–21
thousandths 6
triangles 8–9, 20–21

weighting 14–15